Helping Children See Jesus

ISBN: 978-1-64104-061-7

The Inspiration
of the Scriptures
New Testament Volume 33:
1 & 2 Timothy, Titus, Philemon

Author: R. Iona Lyster
Illustrator: Frances H. Hertzler
Computer Graphic Artist: Ed Olson
Typesetting and Layout: Patricia Pope

© 2018 Bible Visuals International
PO Box 153, Akron, PA 17501-0153
Phone: (717) 859-1131
www.biblevisuals.org

All rights reserved. No part of this publication may be reproduced, stored in a retrieval system or transmitted in any form by any means, electronic, mechanical, photocopy, recording or otherwise, without the prior permission of the publisher, except as provided by USA copyright law.

RELATED ITEMS

To access related items (such as activities, memory verse posters and translated texts) please visit our web store at www.biblevisuals.org and enter 1033 at the top right of the web page. You may need to reduce the zoom setting to get the search box.

FREE TEXT DOWNLOAD

To obtain a FREE printable copy of the English teaching text (PDF format) under Product Format, please scroll down and select Extra–PDF Teacher Text Download. Then under Language select English before clicking the ADD TO CART button to place in your shopping cart. Other languages are available at an additional cost from the Language menu. When checking out, use coupon code XTACSV17 at checkout and click on Apply Coupon to receive the discount on the English text.

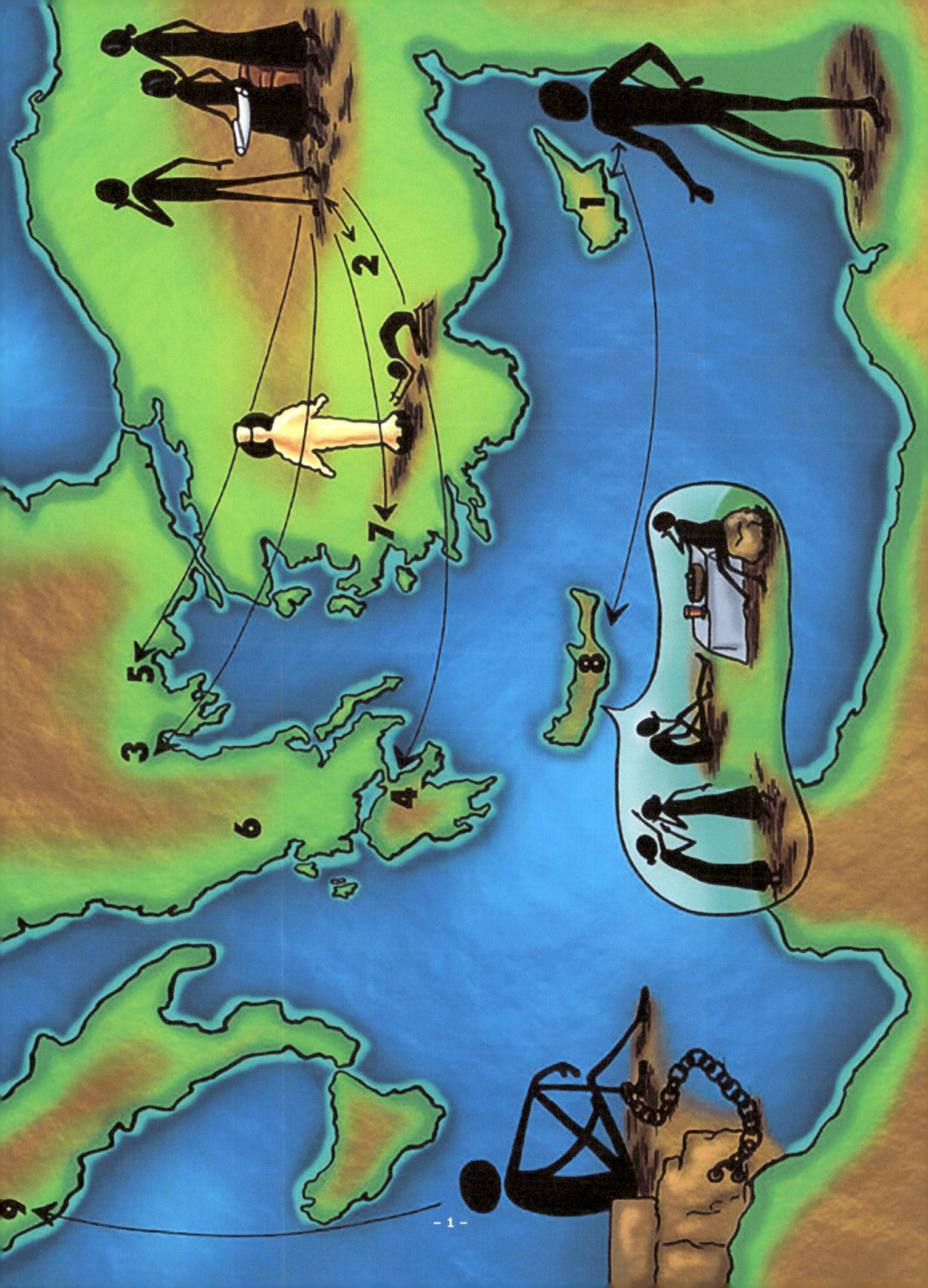

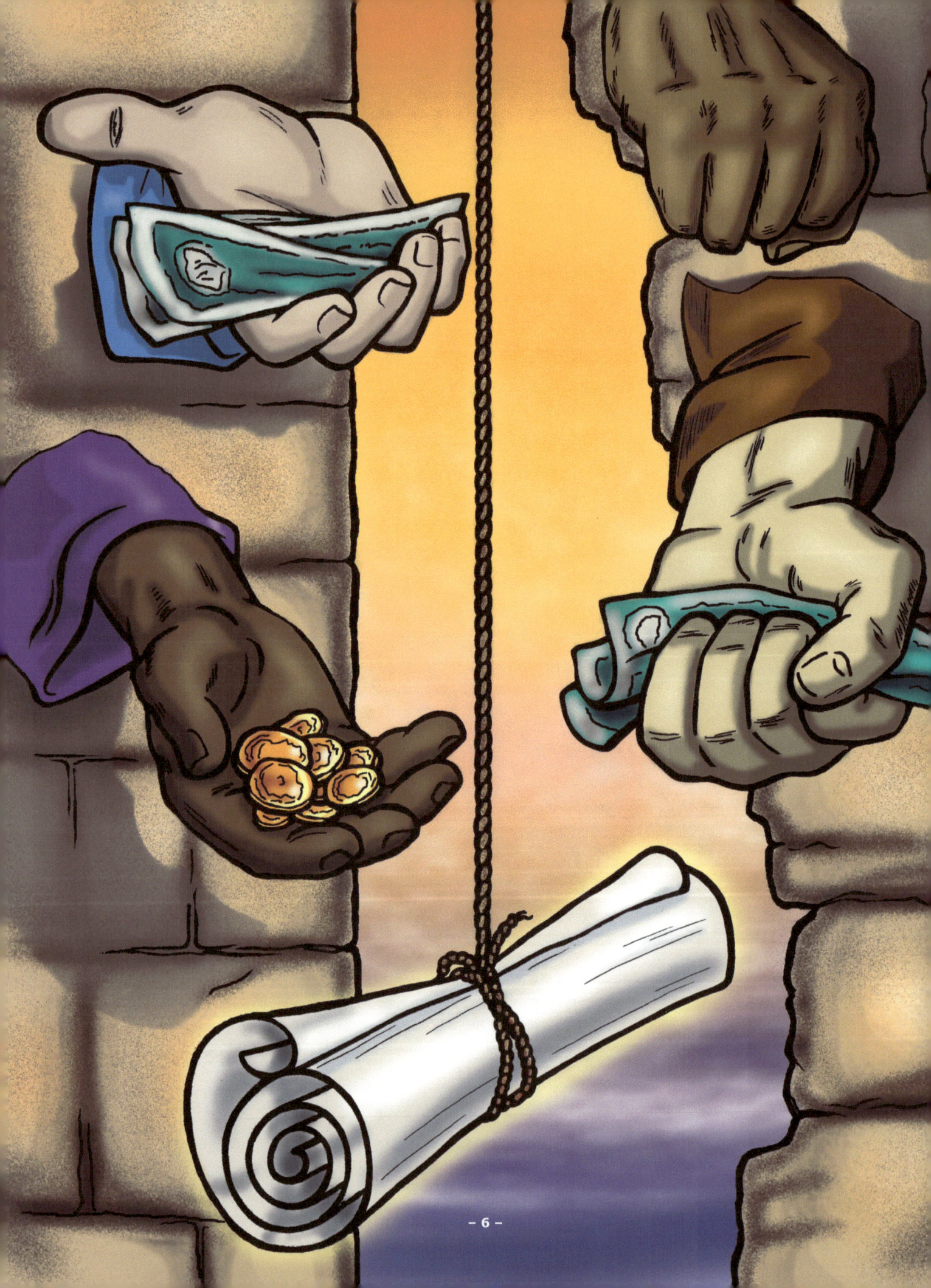

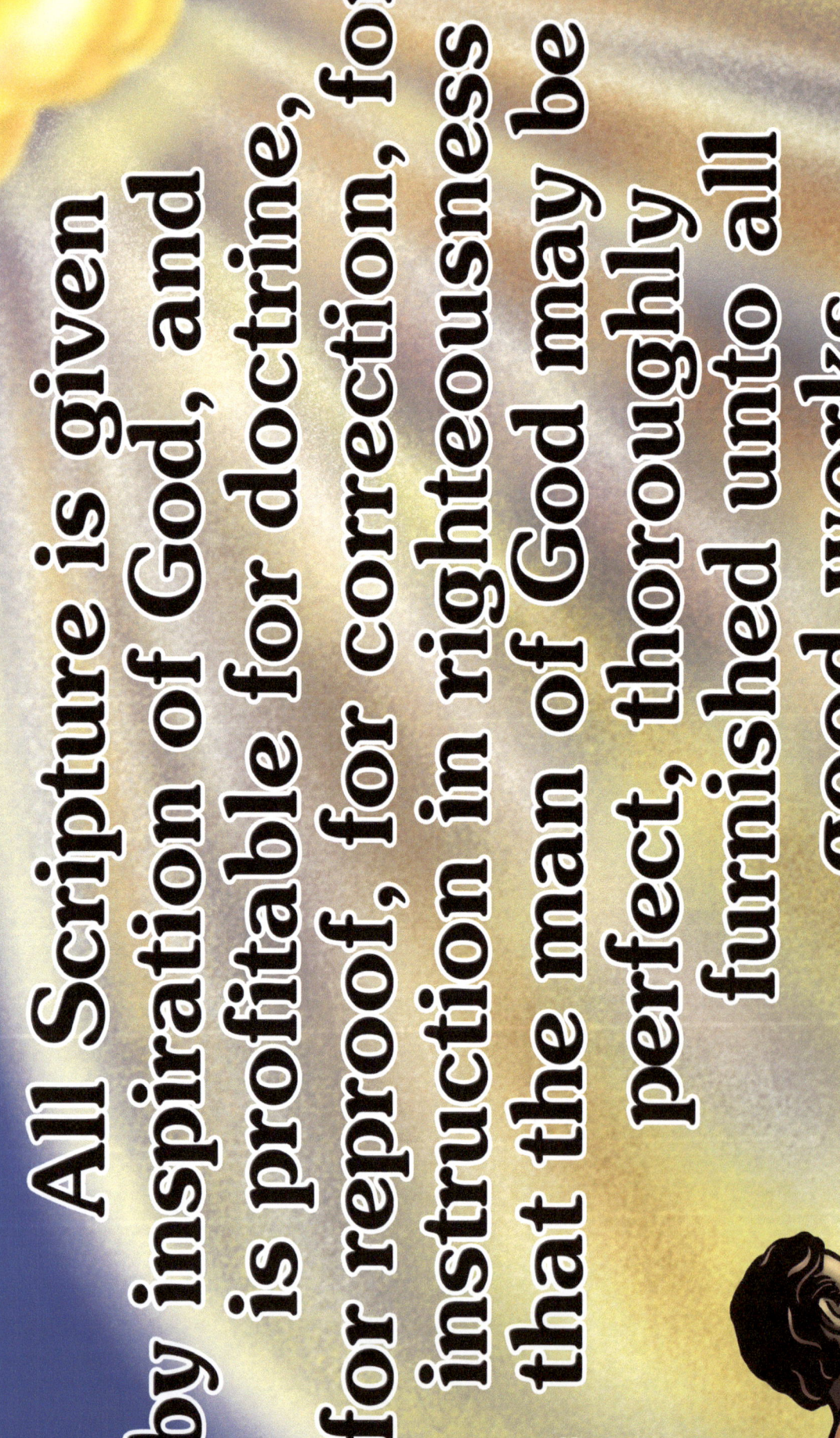

All Scripture is given by inspiration of God, and is profitable for doctrine, for reproof, for correction, for instruction in righteousness that the man of God may be perfect, thoroughly furnished unto all good works.

2 Timothy 3:16, 17

Lesson 1
GOD-INSPIRED TEACHING (DOCTRINE)

NOTE TO THE TEACHER

It is said that in the three letters which the Apostle Paul wrote to Timothy and Titus, he spoke 80 times of the Scripture and its doctrine. Paul was aware that all the apostles would soon be in Heaven. Thereafter believers would be guided entirely by the written word of God. Consequently he emphasized that all final authority rests upon the Bible and its teachings.

The letters addressed to Timothy and Titus are particularly helpful to pastors. However, the apostle included teaching that applies to everyone in the church–including us. These are the truths we shall be studying in this series.

There are numbers on the map which appears on the inside front cover and page 1. If you would like to add the names of the places, they are: #1, Cyprus; #2, Lystra; #3, Thessalonica; #4, Corinth; #5, Philippi; #6, Macedonia; #7, Ephesus; #8, Crete; #9, Rome; #10, Colosse. The symbols on the map will help your students identify the events connected with those places.

The first memory verse (2 Timothy 3:16) begins on the outside back cover and ends on page 16. Verse 17 appears on page 17. By discussing the verses a section at a time, your students should have no difficulty in memorizing them.

Doctrine, which is simply another word for teaching, is important. If your students excel in Bible doctrine, they will be able to combat false doctrine. In addition, Bible teaching *must* affect a person's life. Ask the Spirit of God to apply the truths of the Word to the lives of your students. Remember: the greatest Bible passage on the inspiration of the Scriptures, ends with the idea of doing good works. (See 2 Timothy 3:16-17.) To be a Bible student without living for the Lord is to miss the significance of the Word of God.

Before class time, prepare the note mentioned in the opening part of the lesson.

Scripture to be studied: 1 Timothy 1; 2 Timothy 3:10-4:8

The *aim* of the lesson: To show that because the Bible is God-produced, it is the final authority.

What your students should *know*: That the Scripture, as originally written, has no mistakes but is unconditional truth.

What your students should *feel*: A keen desire to study the Word of God carefully.

What your students should *do*: Study the books of First and Second Timothy.

Wherever the word *doctrine* appears, they should write above it the word *teaching*.

Lesson outline (for the teacher's and students' notebooks):
1. All Scripture is God-produced (2 Timothy 3:16).
2. The Scripture teaches what to believe regarding the Scripture (2 Timothy 2:15; 3:15).
3. The Scripture teaches what to believe regarding salvation (1 Timothy 1:15; 2:4-6; 2 Timothy 1:10; 2:8; 3:15).
4. The Scripture teaches what to believe regarding the future (1 Timothy 4:1-3; 2 Timothy 3:1-5).

The verse to be memorized:

All Scripture is given by inspiration of God and is profitable for doctrine, for reproof, for correction, for instruction in righteousness. (2 Timothy 3:16)

THE LESSON

*I have a problem! Listen to this note I received from a friend: "Will you please meet me at the usual place on Friday at 8:00?"

For more than a year we met at (name a place, pointing towards it). But recently we've met at (name a spot in the opposite direction). I do not know which is the "usual" place. And I do not know when this note was written. Maybe I was supposed to be there last Friday. Or perhaps it is this Friday. Sometimes we have met at 8:00 in the morning. Equally as often we have met at 8:00 at night. How can I know what (s)he means? (Encourage student response. The answer you need is, "You will have to ask the one who wrote the note.")

That is important to remember. When you read something you do not understand, ask the writer what he meant. This is particularly true when you are studying the Bible. God wants you to know what it says and understand what it means. The Holy Spirit of God who wrote the Bible, lives in every true believer in Christ. So, if you belong to Him, you can ask Him to help you understand the truths of His Word. You can also get help in understanding Scripture truth from the comments and writing of godly men and women. (See John 16:13-15.) (*Teacher:* Give students opportunity to pray that the Holy Spirit will teach them through this lesson.)

* Adapted from *Easy-To-Give Object Lessons* by Dr. Charles C. Ryrie. Published by Moody Press, Chicago, IL, 60610. Used by permission. This is a book every teacher should have.

1. ALL SCRIPTURE IS GOD-PRODUCED
2 Timothy 3:16

Of all the books in the world, the Bible is the most marvelous. Forty different men wrote the 66 books of the Bible. Many of them never met each other, for the first book was written 1,600 years before the last book. Yet all agree in everything they wrote. Though there were many men who wrote the Bible, there is only one Author. God, who knows everything, planned the Bible and guided each of the human writers so that each wrote without contradicting the other. It is God who made one Book out of the 66 books.

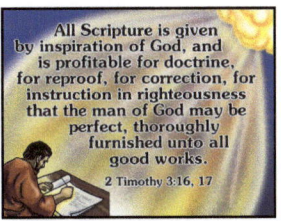

Show Memory Verse Poster

Second Timothy 3:16 tells us that every bit of Scripture is God-inspired. "Inspire" means *to breathe*. When God created the first man, He breathed into Adam the breath of life. When God breathed His thoughts through men, the words they wrote were God's. Since God is really the Author of the Bible, everything the men wrote was exactly right.

We are correct in speaking of this wonderful Book as the Bible (a word meaning *books*). It is right to speak of it as Scripture, or the Scriptures. It is also correct to speak of it as the Word of God, or the living Word of God. By using either of these expressions, we will remember that everything in Scripture is God's word to us. He breathed His messages through men.

Imagine being chosen to write part of the Word of God! How do you suppose the Apostle Paul felt when God gave him that privilege? He *could* have written official papers with big-sounding words. Instead, he simply wrote letters. Some of the letters were addressed to churches. The four letters we shall be studying in this series were written to four men. Like all of Scripture, the letters are for us also. If Paul himself were to tell us why he wrote to Timothy, he might say:

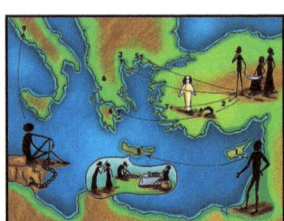

Show Illustration #2

"On my first missionary journey I preached on Cyprus Island (#1 on map) and in Lystra where Timothy lived (#2 on map). Timothy was perfectly prepared to receive the Gospel message. His mother and grandmother had taught him the Old Testament Scriptures from the time he was a child. (See 2 Timothy 1:5; 3:15.) So when I introduced him to the Lord Jesus Christ (see 1 Timothy 1:2; 2 Timothy 1:2), he was ready to receive Him.

"A few years later I returned to Lystra on my second missionary journey. By then Timothy had such a good reputation (1 Timothy 4:14) I invited him to work with Silas and me. (See Acts 16:1-3; 2 Timothy 1:6.) He was timid and not very well. (See 1 Corinthians 16:10; 1 Timothy 5:23.) But he was always obedient, helpful, loyal and dependable. I could send him to take care of some hard things in Thessalonica, Corinth and Philippi (#3, #4, #5 on map). The new churches in those cities needed Timothy's help and encouragement. (See 1 Thessalonians 3:2, 6; 1 Corinthians 4:17; Philippians 2:19-23.)

"When I went to Macedonia (#6) I left Timothy in Ephesus (#7) to care for the churches there. Before the Ephesians heard the Gospel, they worshiped the false goddess, Diana. Those who turned to the true and living God had to be taught how to work together in the church. So God caused me to write the Bible book known as *First Timothy*.

"Later, when I was in a dungeon death cell in Rome (#9), I wrote a second letter to Timothy. He needed to be warned that believers were in danger of being deceived by false teachers. God wanted him (and you!) to know that studying the Word of God is the only way to avoid Satan's trap." (See 2 Timothy 2:15, 26; 3:13-14.)

What did Timothy do when he received Paul's letters? Being young and timid, he may have hesitated at first to instruct the older Ephesian Christians. (See 1 Timothy 4:12; 2 Timothy 1:6-7.) However, he doubtless called together the overseers [leaders] of the churches and read the letter to them. He would have urged them, of course, to share the truths with their congregations.

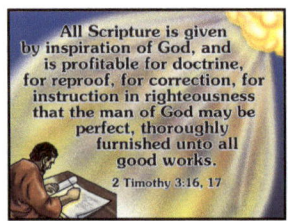

If Timothy could tell us what happened when he received Paul's second letter, is this what he would say?

Show Memory Verse Poster

"When I was only a boy, my mother and grandmother taught me the Old Testament Scriptures. I had always respected these sacred writings. But now, from Paul's letter, I learned this glorious truth: all Scripture is a message breathed by God. (Although Paul's letters to me were not at that time a part of Scripture as they are now, I understood that they were from God.)"

Timothy continued, "So the letter I was holding in my hand was a brand-new portion of God's Word. God had breathed His message through Paul. And, like all of Scripture, it affects my life in these four ways:

1. It teaches me doctrine, so I know what to believe.
2. It reproves me, showing me where I am wrong in my life and thinking.
3. It corrects me, so I know how to get back in the right path.
4. It instructs me in righteousness, so I can know how to live the Christian life.

2. THE SCRIPTURE TEACHES WHAT TO BELIEVE REGARDING THE SCRIPTURE
2 Timothy 2:15; 3:15

Show Illustration #3

"From then on, I studied the Scriptures more carefully, searching for doctrine, reproof, correction, instruction. And I soon found it was like digging in a never-ending gold mine! I studied doctrines first. Since Paul emphasized the importance of God's Word in this second letter, I began with the doctrine of the Scripture. When I wrote it down, the result of my digging looked like this:

Doctrine #1
THE SCRIPTURE

1. The Scripture is *to be studied* (2 Timothy 2:15).
2. The Scripture is *true*, for it is the Word of Truth (2 Timothy 2:15).
3. The Scripture is *holy*–it is an absolutely perfect standard (2 Timothy 3:15).
4. The Scripture is *God's Word*–He breathed it for our guidance (2 Timothy 3:16-17)."

(*Teacher:* It is imperative that your students learn how to find truths for themselves in their daily Bible reading. How you will teach the preceding section and the balance of the lesson depends upon the ability of your students. We strongly urge you to mention the references only. Or, if necessary, read the verses right from the Bible. Direct the thinking of your students so they will be able to pick out the truths and state them simply. Help them to understand that the message which God breathed through Paul is God's message to us as well as to Timothy. Like him, we must study the Word of God so He can guide us day by day. Illustration #2 shows the broad road of life, and the narrow. God's Word guides God's child on the narrow way.)

3. THE SCRIPTURE TEACHES WHAT TO BELIEVE ABOUT SALVATION
1 Timothy 1:15; 2:4-6; 2 Timothy 1:10; 2:8; 3:15

Timothy continued, "Wherever I traveled with the Apostle Paul, I heard him teach the doctrine of salvation. So I was eager to dig into the letters addressed to me, searching for truths about salvation. Here is what I found:

Show Illustration #4

Doctrine #2
SALVATION

1. Jesus Christ came into the world *to save sinners* (1 Timothy 1:15). (The cross in the illustration reminds us that Christ died for our sins. See Isaiah 53:6; 1 Corinthians 15:3-4; 1 Peter 2:24.)
2. God wants *everyone* to be saved (1 Timothy 2:4-6).
3. Saved people have *eternal life* because Christ rose from the dead (2 Timothy 1:10).
4. Salvation comes from *hearing the Word of God* (2 Timothy 3:15). (Do you see in the illustration that some are refusing to listen to God's Word? Such people cannot be saved.)

(*Teacher:* Encourage student discussion.)

4. THE SCRIPTURE TEACHES WHAT TO BELIEVE REGARDING THE FUTURE
1 Timothy 4:1-3; 2 Timothy 3:1-5

"Paul often taught about Christ's coming to take His own people to be with Himself," Timothy would tell us. "I have looked forward to that glorious day. But God knows I am naturally fearful. Maybe that is why He gave warnings in both letters about the terrifying last days on earth before Christ comes. Listen to what God says.

(*Teacher:* Read 1 Timothy 4:1-3; 2 Timothy 3:1-5; 4:1-5.)

"Here are the truths we should remember:

Doctrine #3
THE FUTURE

Before Christ comes in the air for His own,

1. Some who profess Christ will be deceived and turn away from the Christian faith.
2. Some will love themselves.
3. Some will love money and pleasure.
4. Some will not love God.

Show Illustration #5

"The awful things that will happen are no surprise to God," Timothy concludes. "And if we study the Scripture faithfully, we will not be thrown off guard in the evil days. Instead, we are to look for the coming of the Lord Jesus, listening for the trumpet of God. (See 1 Thessalonians 4:16.) And for doing this, God will reward us. (See 2 Timothy 4:8.) The person who *correctly* understands the doctrine of Christ's coming, will use every opportunity to tell the Gospel. God makes this truth perfectly clear." (Read 2 Timothy 4:5.)

In your daily Bible reading study First and Second Timothy. List the doctrines that are taught. Ask the Lord to show you how each truth should affect your life. (For example, the doctrine of Christ's coming for His church should compel us to share the Gospel with others.) Pray that God will make His Word come alive to you.

Lesson 2
GOD-INSPIRED REPROOF AND CORRECTION

Scripture to be studied: All references in outline.

The *aim* of the lesson: To show that God uses His Word to convict, reprove and correct us.

What your students should *know*: The Scripture is the perfect standard and guide for our lives.

What your students should *feel*: A desire to study the Scripture and get their lives in line with it.

What your students should *do*: Accept God's rebukes and put the corrections to work at once. Study these same teachings in the letter to Titus.

Lesson outline (for the teacher's and students' notebooks):

1. The Spirit uses the Scripture to convict (John 16:8, 13; 1 Corinthians 2:12).
2. The Scripture reproves and corrects the love of money (1 Timothy 5:3-10; 6:9-10, 17-19; Titus 1:9-11).
3. The Scripture reproves and corrects foolish talking (1 Timothy 1:3-4; 6:20; 2 Timothy 2:14-16, 23-26; Titus 1:9-11, 13-16).
4. The Scripture reproves and corrects evil desires (2 Timothy 2:22; Titus 2:6; also 1 Timothy 1:18; 6:12; 2 Timothy 2:4-5; 4:7).

The verse to be memorized:

All Scripture is given by inspiration of God and is profitable for doctrine, for reproof, for correction, for instruction in righteousness. (2 Timothy 3:16)

NOTE TO THE TEACHER
Before teaching today's lesson, let your students tell what doctrines they found in their Bible study and how their lives were affected.

THE LESSON

For a few moments, try to put yourself in Timothy's place, remembering these facts:

Although he was rather young, it was his duty to guide the older churches in Ephesus. (The Apostle Paul had given him this responsibility.)

He received two letters from Paul, filled with instruction, rebukes and warnings for the churches.

By nature, he was quite timid.

Now, if you were Timothy, what would you do? (*Teacher:* Encourage student discussion.)

If you knew the letters were from *God*, would you do things differently? (Allow comments.)

Although we cannot know for certain, let us say that Timothy understood the letters were God's Word. Did he visit each church separately? (The churches met in homes, remember.) Or did he call all the churches together? What happened at the meeting? Would it have been like this?

Clearing his throat, Timothy began, "As you know, brothers and sisters, I have studied the Holy Scriptures ever since I was little. These sacred writings are remarkable for a number of reasons. For example, many of the writers never met each other for they lived hundreds of years apart. Some who wrote were poor shepherds. Others were wealthy kings. Some were priests who served God. Others were statesmen. Some wrote of events that took place long before they lived. Others told of things that would happen hundreds–even thousands–of years in the future. Yet it is one Book without any contradictions in what it says."

"It's a miracle Book!" Eldest Brother declared.

"It is!" "It surely is!" the others agreed.

One of the young men said, "What surprises me is that God has kept these writings for us. Some of them must have been written more than a thousand years ago!"

"Yes, they were," Timothy responded. "And this is another reason for calling it a miracle Book. Men have tried to destroy the Word of God, but have been unable to do so."

"Why would anybody want to destroy God's Word?" a bright-eyed boy wanted to know.

"They did not like what it said," Timothy explained.

"Why not?" the boy asked.

"Usually it was because God gave warning that He would punish them for doing sinful things. Once, more than 600 years ago, a certain king (Jehoiakim) received such a warning. After hearing it, he cut up the Book of God (which was written on a scroll) and threw it into the fire. (See Jeremiah 36:1-32.) By destroying the warning, he expected to escape the punishment."

"Did he?"

"No, indeed. He died in disgrace, was dragged out of the city like an animal, and tossed on a junk heap." (See Jeremiah 22:18-19.)

"What about God's Book?"

"God simply wrote it over again. His Word is everlasting."

1. THE SPIRIT USES THE SCRIPTURE TO CONVICT
John 16:8, 13; 1 Corinthians 2:12

Show Illustration #6

The boy's father spoke up. "Son, you have watched me build many walls. What do I use for a guide so the wall will be straight?"

"A plumb line."

"Right! What makes the plumb line hang straight?"

"The weight on it."

"Suppose I built a crooked wall. Would the wall be all right if I destroyed the plumb line?"

"Of course not," the boy laughed. "The wall would still be crooked."

"Exactly. And even though the wicked King Jehoiakim tried to destroy the Word of God–the very thing which showed he was out of line–he was still sinful. I trust, son, you will always be wise enough to check every part of your life by Scripture, God's eternal plumb line and follow its direction."

Timothy declared, "That's good advice for all of us."

"Exactly *how* do we check our lives by Scripture?" an alert young man asked.

"God answers that in Paul's second letter to me," Timothy answered. (Show 2 Timothy 3:16, back cover and Illustration 16.) "First, we are to check whatever we are taught, making certain it is according to the teaching [doctrine] of Scripture. Teachers sometimes change their ideas. They may teach one thing today, quite another later on. (*Teacher:* Mention some false teaching that your students may have had. If, for example, they have been taught the evolutionary theory, give them Scripture verses which prove God created man.) Man's ideas may change. God never changes. His Word never changes. You can always depend on it for it is truth. (See John 17:17.)

"In addition to checking our teaching with Scripture, we are to check our thoughts, our attitudes, our speech, our companions, our desires. When we read God's Word, He will show us the crooked, wrong things we should stop doing. He will also show us how to change our way of living."

2. THE SCRIPTURE REPROVES AND CORRECTS THE LOVE OF MONEY
1 Timothy 5:3-10; 6:9-10, 17-19; Titus 1:9-11

Timothy fastened one end of a long, heavy cord to the ceiling. He tied a Scripture scroll to the loose end.

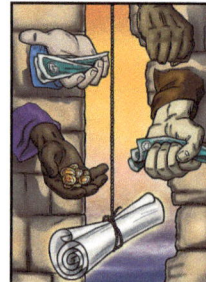

Show Illustration #7

Bright-eyed boy announced, "I know what that is. It's the Word of God plumb line."

"Right you are," Timothy responded. "In Paul's two letters to me, God mentions certain wrongs that any of us may be guilty of. Let's check the plumb line of God's Word to see if our lives are right. Elder Brother, will you please read this one which I have marked?"

Elder Brother read, " 'The love of money is the root of all kinds of sin. Some have turned from the faith because of their love for money' (1 Timothy 6:10)." He paused, looking embarrassed. "This is serious," he said slowly, tugging his beard. "The youngest person here, as well as the oldest, may love money and the things money can buy. I confess this is a problem with me. No matter how much money I have or how many things I have, I always want more–for myself, of course. I am guilty of loving money. Oh, I'm so ashamed!" Elder Brother sat down, burying his face in his hands.

"I did not know this was a problem with you," Timothy said kindly. "But God knew. And you have accepted His rebuke, admitting that your life does not match the plumb line of His Word. Remember, however, that God's Word also corrects us by showing how to do right. Listen to this: '. . . Have a kind heart . . . Do good . . . Give to those in need. Be ready to share . . .' (1 Timothy 6:11, 18.) Our attitude towards money must be constantly checked by these teachings of God's Word. We must be *giving* Christians–not grasping for ourselves."

3. THE SCRIPTURE REPROVES AND CORRECTS FOOLISH TALKING
1 Timothy 1:3-4; 6:20; 2 Timothy 2:14-16, 23-26; Titus 1:9-11, 13-16

Timothy continued, "In these two letters, God mentions another matter which affects those of any age."

"What's that?" Bright-eyed boy wanted to know.

"Foolish talking," Timothy replied.

"You mean I can't joke and have fun?"

Show Illustration #8

"No, that is not what He speaks of here. He says there are many who do not know or believe the truths of His Word. They talk a lot trying to impress others with their knowledge. They love to argue with Christians, hoping to get them to turn away from God. God says we are not to pay attention to them. He says it is foolish to have arguments with unbelievers who do not know what they are talking about. And God rebukes those who do it."

"That really hits me," Alert Young Man declared. "I'm forever arguing with others who do not know God or His Word. Lately I have had a feeling that some of them have turned even farther away from the Lord."

"God says that is exactly what will happen," Timothy said. (Read 2 Timothy 2:16.)

"So God has rebuked me. What can I do to correct this habit?"

"Study the Word of God. (See 2 Timothy 2:15.) By studying His Word earnestly, you can become a good workman for Him. Later, when you are prepared to teach, be gentle to those who are against you. God may change their hearts so they will turn to Him."

Alert Young Man concluded, "So, instead of arguing foolishly, I must study the Word of God carefully. That will not be easy for me. But it will be worth it if I shall be able to teach the truths of God someday."

4. THE SCRIPTURE REPROVES AND CORRECTS EVIL DESIRES
2 Timothy 2:22; Titus 2:6; also 1 Timothy 1:18; 6:12; 2 Timothy 2:4-5; 4:7

Timothy said, "God says something else to the young: 'Turn your back on sinful things young people do.' But there is a truth here for everyone."

Show Illustration #9

Timothy continued, "When God wrote through Paul to you Ephesians, He commanded: 'Put on the whole armor of God.' (See Ephesians 6:10-18.) He knows that the Christian life is a constant battle. When we fail to use that armor, Satan's darts hit us. We do not live pure lives. We are proud, angry–and useless. Any sinful desire is out of line with the plumb line of God's Word. God commands us to turn from sin and go after what is right. By studying the Word of God–and by using it–we can defeat Satan, our enemy. For God's Word is the sword of the Spirit."

According to the Word of God, is your life straight? Do you have the right attitude about money? Are you studying God's Word rather than arguing with unbelievers? Do you have good, pure, right desires? If not, will you confess your sin to God right now? Then, after prayer, write in your notebook what you plan to do this week to get in line with God's Word.

Before our next meeting, see what the book of Titus says about these matters. (See the lesson outline.)

Lesson 3
GOD-INSPIRED INSTRUCTION FOR RIGHT LIVING

Scripture to be studied: Titus 1-3

The *aim* of the lesson: To show that good doctrine and good works are connected. The Christian must have both.

> **What your students should *know*:** God wants His children to know and do His will.
>
> **What your students should *feel*:** Zeal to know God's will for daily living.
>
> **What your students should *do*:** Determine what ungodly practices they must turn from and what godly things they should do.

Lesson outline (for the teacher's and students' notebooks):

1. The Scripture teaches how to live the Christian life (Matthew 4:1-10; Psalm 119:105).
2. We should be *eager* to do good works (Titus 2:11-15).
3. We should be *ready* to do any good work (Titus 3:1-7).
4. We should *constantly* do good works (Titus 3:8-11, 14; compare 1:10-11).

The verse to be memorized:

> *All Scripture is given by inspiration of God and is profitable for doctrine, for reproof, for correction, for instruction in righteousness.* (2 Timothy 3:16)

THE LESSON

A Christian must read the Bible! If you cannot read, get someone to read it to you. If you do not have a Bible, ask the Lord to provide one for you. Save your money so you can pay for it when He sends it. It is extremely important that you read the Word of God faithfully.

*I have here something we all enjoy eating. (*Teacher:* Use a candy bar, sugar cane, sticky rice, tortilla, or whatever your people like for a special treat.) Who will offer to eat some of it as fast as possible? (Allow student to do this.) That is the way some people read their Bibles. They rush through without taking time to think about what they are reading. How much do you suppose they get from it? . . . If you are going to learn from your Bible reading, you must not be in a hurry. Take time when you read God's Word.

> **NOTE TO THE TEACHER**
>
> The central idea of Paul's letter to Titus is expressed in a word which appears in every chapter: *work*. Paul stresses the importance of salvation by grace in 2:11-14 and 3:4-8. Each time he concludes with an emphasis on good works. In this short letter, God commands the believer (1) to be zealous of good works (2:14); (2) to be ready to work (3:1); (3) to be careful to do good works (3:8); and (4) to learn to devote himself to good works (3:14). God requires each saved person to live as a good representative of Christ–wisely, righteously, godly–in this world (2:12).
>
> Your students may forget what you teach, Teacher. They will remember how you live. Is your life God-like?

Now who will eat the rest of this treat slowly? (Have volunteer eat slowly, chewing well.) This is the proper way to eat. It is also the correct way to read the Word of God. Take time to think about what you read. In other words, meditate. The Bible itself stresses the importance of this. (See Psalm 1:2; 119:97.)

* Adapted from *Easy-To-Give Object Lessons* by Dr. Charles C. Ryrie. Published by Moody Press, Chicago, IL 60610. Used by permission.

This Book, produced by God Himself, is God-inspired. (Show 2 Timothy 3:16 on back cover and Illustration 16.) It is a treasure from which we get lasting profit. It teaches us doctrine so we know what to believe. It reproves us, showing us where we are wrong in our lives and thoughts. It corrects us by getting us back to the right way of living and thinking. And it instructs us so we can know God's will for our daily lives. To get this help for successful living, we must study and meditate on the Word of God each day. (See Joshua 1:8.)

1. THE SCRIPTURE TEACHES HOW TO LIVE THE CHRISTIAN LIFE
Matthew 4:1-10; Psalm 119:105

Like a light on a dark path, God's Word shows us exactly how to live the Christian life. (See Psalm 119:105, 130; Proverbs 4:18.) If we know the Word of God and follow its teaching, we will be kept in the way of God. But Satan will do everything he can to get us out of God's way. He even tried to get the Lord Jesus to go his way rather than God's.

Show Illustration #10

He suggested that Jesus should feed Himself by making bread from stones. Then he urged Christ to cast Himself off the top of the temple wall, allowing angels to take care of Him. Again Satan tempted our Lord to take over the kingdoms of the world and reign.

The Lord Jesus Christ might have reasoned that people would turn to God if they knew He made stones into bread, or saw angels caring for Him when He dropped from a great height, or saw Him taking the world kingdoms for Himself. But He knew from the Word of God that these were not the will of God for His life. So each time Satan tempted him to do wrong, the Lord Jesus answered by quoting from God's Word. (See Matthew 4:4, 7, 10.)

Every bit of Scripture was important to the Lord Jesus Christ. He said that each word, even every letter would be fulfilled exactly as it is written. "Not one jot or one tittle will pass away . . . until it has all been done," He said. (See Matthew 5:18.) A *jot* is the smallest letter in the Hebrew alphabet. (In English, it looks like an apostrophe. (*Teacher:* Point it out in the illustration. In addition, show an apostrophe in your Bible so your students will see how small it is in relation to the rest of the type.) The *tittle* is the tiny mark that changes one Hebrew letter to another. (*Teacher:* The Hebrew letters in the illustration are Beth and Caph which may appear in your Bible above Psalm 119:9 and 81. The tittle is the bottom right of the letter Beth. The other letters are Daleth and Resh. These are above Psalm 119:25 and 153. The tittle is the top right of Daleth. When set in type, these differences are tiny. But even these very small parts of letters in Scripture are of utmost importance, Christ said.)

Christ Jesus accepted all the Scripture as His guide for life on earth. Any Christian who does as He did will also receive instruction from God Himself. (See Psalm 32:8.)

2. WE SHOULD BE *EAGER* TO DO GOOD WORKS
Titus 2:11-15

Some years after the death and resurrection of Christ Jesus, the Apostle Paul wrote to a young preacher named Titus. Let us suppose that Paul could be here to tell us why he wrote that letter. Maybe he would say it this way:

"On my first missionary journey, I preached on Cyprus Island (#1 on map), Titus's home. He was born into the family of God through my ministry. So I always thought of him as another of my sons in the Christian faith. (See Titus 1:4.) He was strong, young, courageous, an energetic leader, and a reliable helper. He was the kind who offered to help even without being asked! (See 2 Corinthians 8:16-17.)

"At about the same time I wrote the first letter to Timothy, I wrote also to Titus. I had left him on the Isle of Crete (See map #8.) to care for the churches there. (See Titus 1:5.) The Cretans had poor reputations. They were liars, lazy, and they ate too much. (See Titus 1:12-13.) These bad habits even affected the Christians. They had to learn the correct way of living the Christian life.

Show Illustration #11A

"God caused me to write this message to Titus for the Cretans: 'You must turn away from ungodliness and evil desires. You must live honorable, God-fearing lives. While living this new life, you are to be looking for the glorious appearing of our great God and Saviour, Jesus Christ. [He is coming for us with a shout, the voice of the archangel, and the trump of God.] He gave Himself for us to rescue us from our evil way of life. Because He has made us clean and pure, we should be eager to live good lives.' (See Titus 2:12-14.)

Show Illustration #11B

"When the lazy, greedy men (see lower part of illustration) in Crete heard this part of the letter, they knew at once that God had rebuked them. The farmers who had been selfishly keeping all their crops for themselves, were also rebuked. They understood that from now on they were to allow some of their grain to be left for the poor to gather. They accepted the rebuke and got into the correct way of living. And they did it eagerly because they realized that the Lord Jesus Christ might come at any time."

3. WE SHOULD BE *READY* TO DO ANY GOOD WORK
Titus 3:1-7

If Titus himself could tell us what he did when he received the letter from Paul, do you think it would be like this:

"I went from house to house visiting the congregations which met in those houses. I let the Cretans see with their own eyes this message from God. They studied the letter carefully. Then one of the church elders exclaimed, 'According to this, we are to put our Christian teaching to work every day of our lives. And we are to do it in practical ways. We must obey the leaders of our country, even if they do not believe the Christian Gospel. We must not say anything that would harm them or anyone else. We must not argue with others, as we did before we trusted in Christ. We used to be jealous and wanted what belonged to others. Now we must be gentle and kind–as God has been to us. These are commands from God, brothers.' "

"You are right," I (Titus) replied.

Show Illustration #12

"God showed His love and kindness by saving us through Christ's death. Our sins are cleansed by the precious blood of Christ. We have been born into the family of God. We have everlasting life. God's Holy Spirit lives within us. Because all of this is so, we are ready to do good works. Doing good could never save us. But we do good because we *are* saved."

This was doubtless brand-new teaching for the Cretans. They were learning from God Himself that what a person believes affects his life. When you live according to right doctrine, you are like those dressed up for a special occasion. If you are eating dinner at the home of a government official, you dress one way. If you are planting crops, you dress another way. For swimming, you wear something entirely different. You dress according to the occasion. Just so, what you know about Bible doctrine affects the way you live.

4. WE SHOULD *CONSTANTLY* DO GOOD WORKS
Titus 3:8-11, 14; compare 1:10-11

Titus read the last part of the letter emphatically: " 'Those who have believed in God must take the lead constantly in doing good works.' "

A leading elder said with surprise, "I see it clearly now. To know God and the teaching about God is like the root of a tree. From the root must come fruit–good works. A root without fruit is good for nothing. Fruit without a root can only be artificial fruit. I have to know right doctrine first. Then I'll do good works constantly."

Show Illustration #13A

"That is exactly right," Titus declared. "Now listen to this: 'Do not argue with people about foolish questions . . . This does not help anyone and is of no use.'

Show Illustration 13B

Earlier in the letter we are warned not to listen to the foolish teaching of the unbelieving Jews. They teach nonsense in order to get money! (See top of illustration. Compare Titus 1:10-11.) They reject the truth of God and want to get Christians to follow them. Now remember: no arguing about foolish questions; no listening to foolish teaching of unbelievers. Instead, be careful to do good things all the time."

Some of the Cretans immediately wanted to know, "Exactly what good things should we do?"

An elder answered, "We must learn to work hard, instead of being lazy. We must give to others who need help, instead of being greedy. We must always take the leading in doing good works." (See Titus 3:13-14.)

If you had lived on the Isle of Crete, what would you have stopped doing after hearing God's message? What would you have begun to do? (Allow class discussion.)

Since you are not a Cretan, what do you think God wants *you* to stop doing? Will you list those things in your notebook? Has God been speaking to you today, telling you the good works He wants you to do? Will you list those in your notebook? Then we shall pray together asking the Lord to help you begin working on these this week, starting today.

NOTE TO THE TEACHER

Although the letter addressed to Philemon is the last of the four books to be studied in this series, it was doubtless written before the other three. First Timothy and Titus were written about five years later (probably in AD 67). About a year thereafter, when Paul was again a Roman prisoner, he wrote his last Bible letter, Second Timothy. Shortly after this he was put to death–by beheading, it is believed.

You will want to emphasize the importance of the two memory verses, on which this lesson is built. Pray that the truths declared in these verses will grip your students and affect their lives forever.

Lesson 4
THE GOD-INSPIRED SCRIPTURES COMPLETELY EQUIP CHRISTIANS

Scripture to be studied: 2 Timothy 3:16-17, all references in the lesson, Philemon.

The *aim* of the lesson: To show that all Scripture profits the Christian and affects his life for good.

What your students should *know*: Like all weapons, the Scriptures must be used in order to be effective.

What your students should *feel*: An eagerness to have the Word of God change their lives.

What your students should *do*: Promise God to study His Word. List any "good works" they believe He wants them to do. Decide what should be changed in their daily living.

Lesson outline (for the teacher's and students' notebooks):
1. All Scripture is profitable (2 Timothy 3:16).
2. Scripture provides what the Christian needs to be completely upright (2 Timothy 3:17).
3. Scripture completely equips the Christian for good works (2 Timothy 2:2; 4:2, 9, 13, 21).
4. Scripture affects daily living (Philemon 1-25).

The verses to be memorized:

All Scripture is given by inspiration of God and is profitable for doctrine, for reproof, for correction, for instruction in righteousness: that the man of God may be perfect, thoroughly furnished unto all good works.

(2 Timothy 3:16-17)

THE LESSON

Almost everyone enjoys receiving letters. Timothy, in the long ago, was glad when the Apostle Paul wrote to him. And he immediately shared his letters with the Ephesians. We have no way of knowing all that happened when Timothy and the Ephesians studied the second letter together. Do you think it may have been like this?

1. ALL SCRIPTURE IS PROFITABLE
2 Timothy 3:16

Show Memory Verse Poster

"Look!" Elder Brother exclaimed. "It says here that the Word of God is a *profit* to us. We will enjoy making a profit. It would be a great day for us if we could trade a _____ for a _____." (*Teacher:* Name two objects known to your students–the second being of much more value than the first.)

A young businessman declared, "I would surely like to make that kind of profit!" The Ephesians laughed, nodding their heads in agreement.

Show Illustration #14

Alert Young Man added, "Before I was a Christian, I used to work at the theater here in Ephesus. You know, of course, that as many as 25,000 people attend the plays. It takes a long time for the men in charge to count all the profits they make! We were paid such a little that it used to bother me to see all the money they had. Now I see that we have a profit that is really worthwhile. According to this message from God, His Word gives us lasting profit. If I study it and follow its teachings, it will guide me all my life. That is certainly far better than money profits which disappear!"

One of the leading elders tugged his beard, saying, "We who are older remember the day the idol-makers rioted here in Ephesus. (See Acts 19:23-41.) Our city was known around the world for its great temple of the goddess, Diana. When the Apostle Paul preached the Gospel here, many of us turned to the Saviour and stopped worshiping Diana. This terrified the idol-makers. They realized that people would stop buying their images of the goddess. And they would lose their profits. So they rioted. Making a profit has always been important to us Ephesians. But I have learned an important truth from this message from God. All of Scripture gives me lasting profit. It teaches me what to believe. It points out the wrong things I am doing. It corrects me and gets me back into the right ways. And it instructs me so I can know how to live the Christian life. This kind of profit lasts forever."

"It does." "It really does," the Ephesians all agreed.

One of the gray-haired men spoke up, saying, "As you know, I am in the money-lending business. When we Jews lend to foreigners, we are allowed to make a profit. (See Exodus 22:25; Deuteronomy 23:19-20.) I really watch carefully when a man comes to repay his loan. First he counts out the exact amount he borrowed. Then he adds more coins–maybe two, or ten, or even a hundred. This is my profit. But I see now that even more important is the profit that comes to me from the amazing Word of God. I must study it more."

"Me, too," each Ephesian murmured.

2. SCRIPTURE PROVIDES WHAT THE CHRISTIAN NEEDS TO BE COMPLETELY UPRIGHT
2 Timothy 3:17

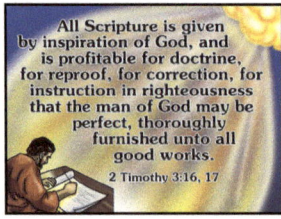
Show Memory Verse Poster

"But did you notice this, brothers?" Timothy asked, pointing to the letter. "In addition to being a profit to us, the Word of God makes us perfect."

"Perfect? How can that be? I will never be perfect!" Alert Young Man declared.

Timothy explained, "In the Old Testament Scriptures God spoke of Noah as a perfect man. He also commanded Abraham to be perfect. (See Genesis 6:9; 17:1.) Yet both men sinned. However, when they obeyed God and lived as He instructed, they were completely upright–which is the meaning of the word *perfect*. We too are complete and upright when we know the Word of God and live according to its teachings."

Show Illustration #15

Timothy continued, "In the letter which Paul wrote to you Ephesians, he spoke of the Word of God as *the Sword of the Spirit*. (See Ephesians 6:17.) So, in addition to knowing God's Word and following its teachings, we must use it."

"How do we use it?" a young boy wanted to know.

"Just as a soldier uses his sword," Timothy explained. "A sword protects the soldier by keeping his enemy away from him. But if the enemy does get close, the soldier attacks with his sword. Our enemy is Satan. He is always trying to get us to do wrong. But if we know and obey what God says in His Word, we will refuse to do what Satan tempts us to do. But we cannot use the Word of God unless we know it. We learn to know it by reading it and thinking about it (meditating). If we also memorize it, we will be able to quote it when Satan tempts us. This is *using* the Word of God. It is exactly what the Lord Jesus did when Satan tempted Him. So, like Him, we must use this Sword of the Spirit," Timothy concluded, holding up the Scripture.

3. SCRIPTURE COMPLETELY EQUIPS THE CHRISTIAN FOR GOOD WORKS
2 Timothy 2:2; 4:2, 9, 13, 21

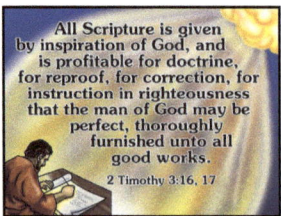
Show Memory Verse Poster

Alert Young Man spoke again. "I see now that we can be complete and upright Christians by knowing the Word of God and following its teachings. But the Bible will do even more for us: it will equip us to do all good works."

"What kind of good works?" a timid brother wanted to know.

"Preaching and teaching," Timothy answered. (See 2 Timothy 4:2; 2:2.)

"Oh, I could never do that!" Timid Brother exclaimed.

"Doing something helpful is also a good work," Timothy said encouragingly.

"Like what?" Timid Brother asked.

"Visiting someone in prison. (See 2 Timothy 4:9, 21.) Or taking a coat, a book, or a copy of the Scriptures to someone who needs one of these is a good work." (See 2 Timothy 4:13. *Teacher:* The word *parchments* doubtless refers to the skins on which certain Old Testament Scriptures were written.) Timothy continued, "Sometimes in our Bible study we learn exactly what God wants us to do. At other times, we will know in our hearts what God is telling us to do. Either way, we will be completely equipped to do good works if we study all of Scripture."

4. SCRIPTURE AFFECTS DAILY LIVING
Philemon 1-25

Show Illustration #16

Timothy continued, "God wants us who are His children to know what we should be and do. So He has breathed all Scripture for our profit. It is His breath that gives life to His Book. And His living Word is meant to affect our daily living. Those who study God's Word and follow its teachings, live gloriously, even in the hard places of life. There are others in the family of God who do not take time to read or study the Bible. They decide for themselves how to live the Christian life, rather than learning from God. They will get to Heaven because they have trusted in the Saviour. But, oh, how hard it is for them! They make mistakes, they stumble, many fall along the way. If they would read and use the Word of God, all of life would be easier."

The Ephesians all agreed.

"I was with the Apostle Paul when he wrote another message from God," Timothy added. "Paul was in prison in Rome at the time. (He is again a prisoner, as you know.) Even in jail Paul preached the Gospel. One who received the Saviour at that time was Onesimus. We learned that he was a slave who had run away from his owner, Philemon. Paul liked Onesimus. And Onesimus liked Paul so much that he helped Paul a great deal. But Paul knew that Onesimus really belonged to Philemon. So he explained to Onesimus that he would have to return to Philemon in Colosse 700 miles away. 'I can't go back there,' Onesimus insisted. 'Philemon will kill me!'

"'If he kills you, it will be what you deserve,' Paul answered. 'You knew before you ran away that your punishment could be death. Philemon is a Christian. Now you are also a Christian. I shall write a letter for you to take to him. We can trust the Lord to do whatever is best.'

"It was interesting to watch Paul as he wrote that letter," Timothy said. "Frequently he stopped and prayed. What he wrote was really from God. He said, 'In my prayers I always thank God for you, Philemon . . . Although I could order you to do something which I think is right, I am not doing that. Instead, I am appealing to your love . . . for Onesimus, my child in the Christian faith. He has been useless to you in the past. But now he is going to be useful. I am sending him back to you. Will you receive him as my son? You lost him for a time. Now you will have him back for good, not only as a slave, but as a Christian brother . . . Welcome him as you would welcome me. If he has wronged you or owes you anything, put it to my account. I have written this with my own hand. I, Paul, will repay you.' "

Timothy went on, "Imagine that! Paul, the greatest of missionaries, asked to have charged to himself the debt of Onesimus, the slave. And all of Paul's good reputation was to be put to Onesimus's account. I have often wondered what Onesimus thought as he trudged those 700 miles to Colosse. When he got there, do you think he first apologized to Philemon for having sinned against him? Or did he give his testimony, telling how he had turned to the Lord for salvation of sin? Did he promise to make things right with his master?" (*Teacher:* Have class discussion, encouraging them to tell how Onesimus might have felt.)

We can imagine that one of the rich Ephesian slave-owners said, "I wonder how Philemon felt when he saw Onesimus? Was his first thought to kill him, as he deserved? Did he refuse Paul's letter? Or did he grab it? Did he forgive Onesimus immediately? Or did it take a long time? Did he treat all of his slaves more kindly after this?" The man looked perplexed, wondering what he himself would do. (*Teacher:* Try to have your students express how such a letter should have affected Philemon's life.)

Because the little letter to Philemon is part of God's Word, it is also for you. Is there some particular teaching you need? Some reproof? Some correction? Some instruction in right living? Is there some good work you should do for someone else? Do you have attitudes that should be changed? (*Teacher:* Ask questions appropriate for your group. Encourage students to list in their notebooks the matters God has called to their attention. Pray together that God will help them to live in line with His Word.)

www.ingramcontent.com/pod-product-compliance
Lightning Source LLC
Chambersburg PA
CBHW060807090426
42736CB00002B/191